Dominique Fashion Design Sketchbook

DOMINIQUE FASHION DESIGN SKETCHBOOK

100 SINGLE-SIDED CROQUIS FASHION FIGURE POSE TEMPLATES FOR SKETCHING GARMENT DESIGNS

DOMINIQUE HENRICHON

Dominique Fashion Design Sketchbook

ISBN 978-1-928242-15-4

Published by InvestEbooks in 2020

www.investebooks.com

Johannesburg, South Africa

Foreword

The Dominique Fashion Design Sketchbook provides accomplished fashion designers and aspiring garment designers with fashion sketchpads of lightly drawn croquis models in different poses. Fashion designers do not have to spend time on drawing the croquis models first and can concentrate on their core capability - to design and sketch garments.

There are 100 different croquis model templates, two per page, with blank pages in between, so that there will be no bleed-through to the next drawing. The model poses are lightly drawn so that you can sketch the fashion clothes over them.

This fashion design sketchbook is an indispensable tool for quickly creating your own fashion designs as well as for building up a portfolio of designs to professionally present to admission panels or prospective employers.

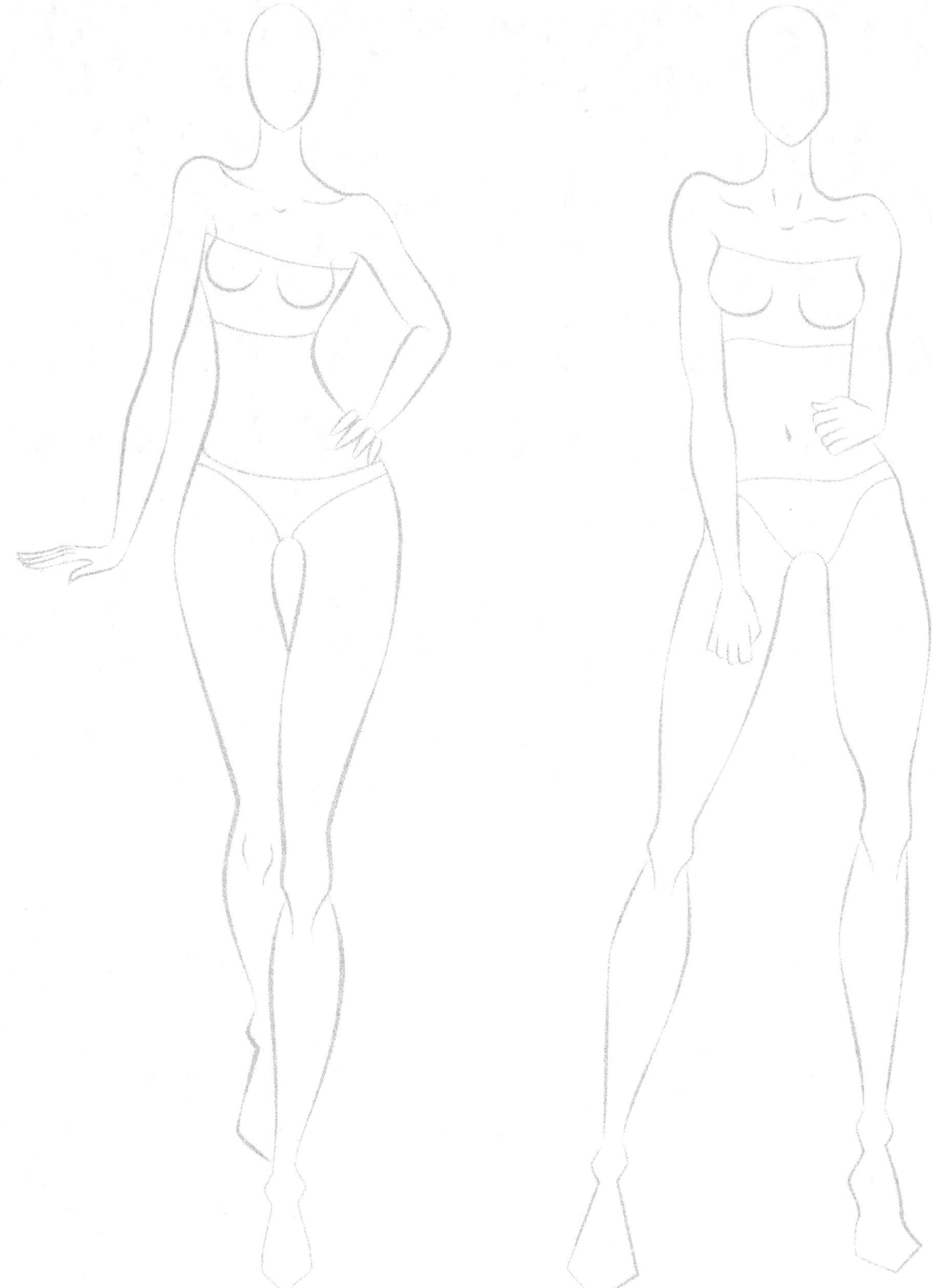

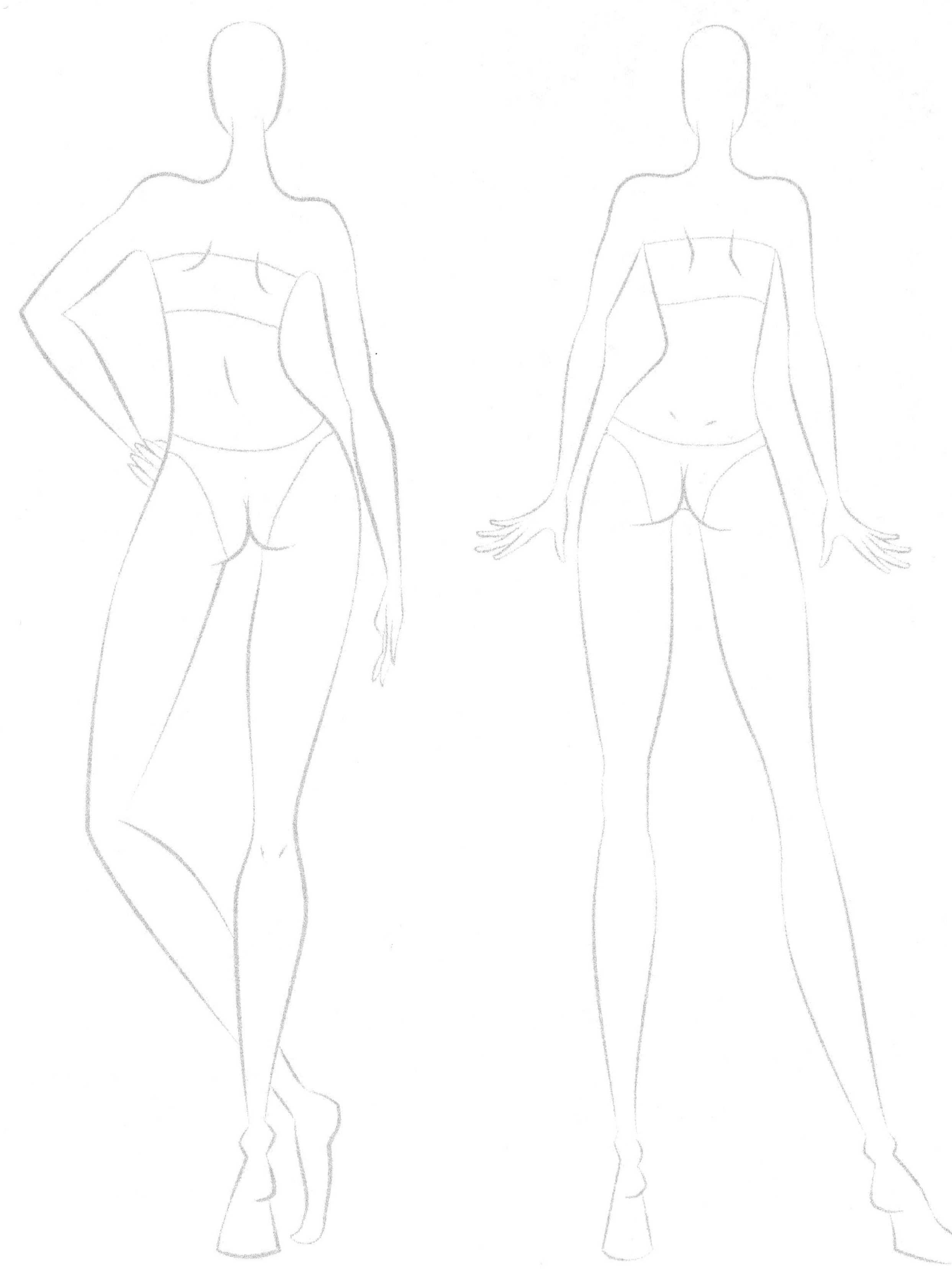

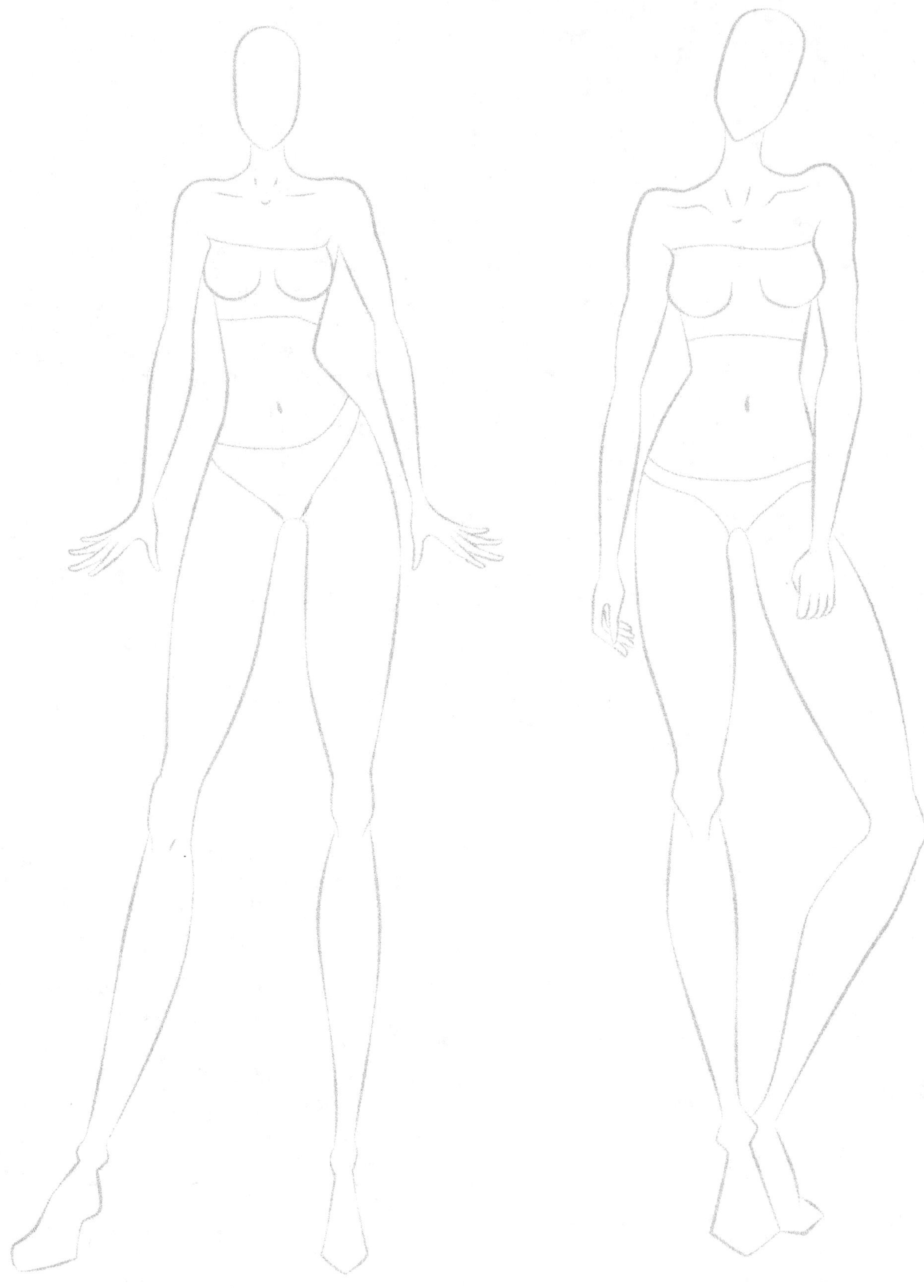

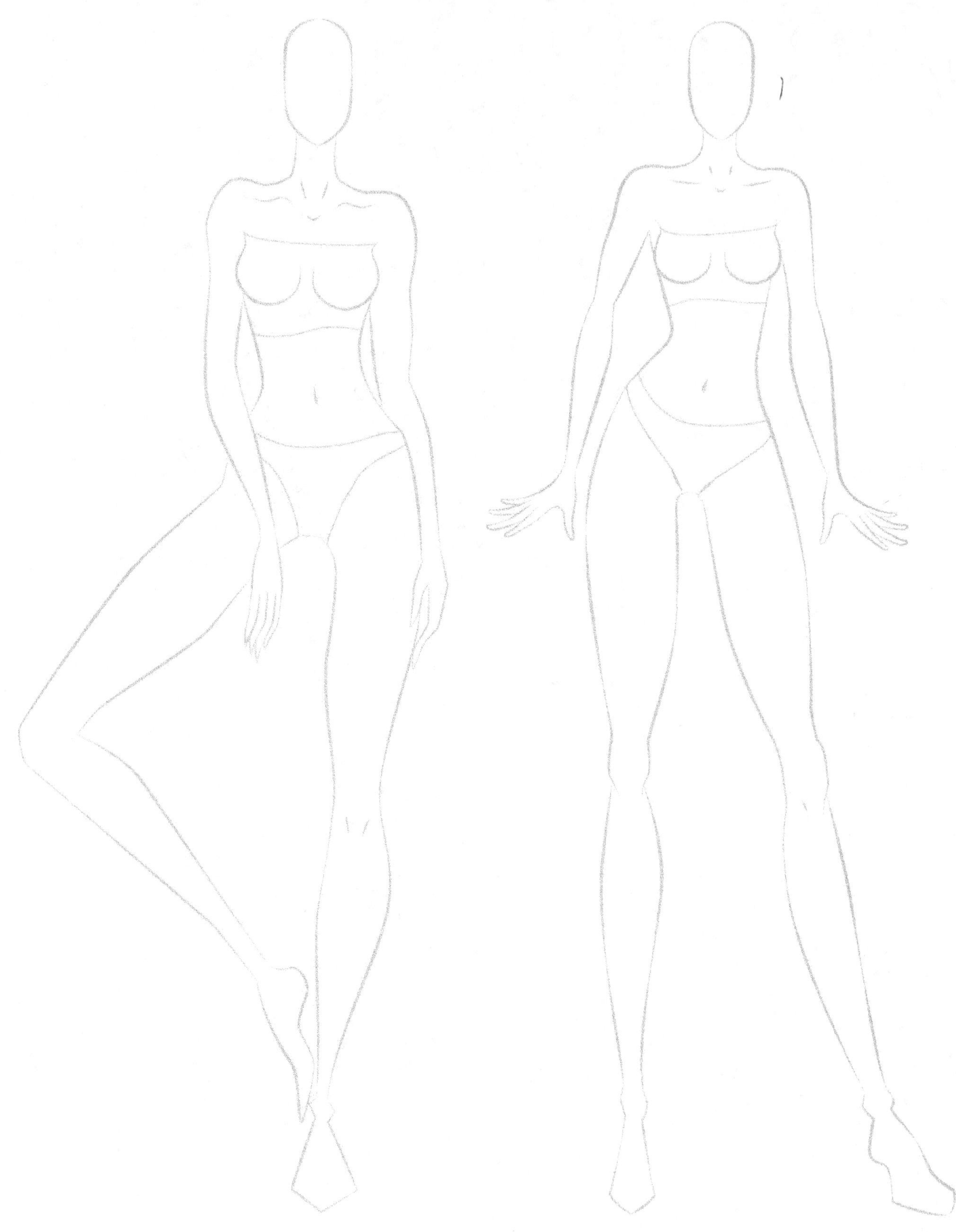

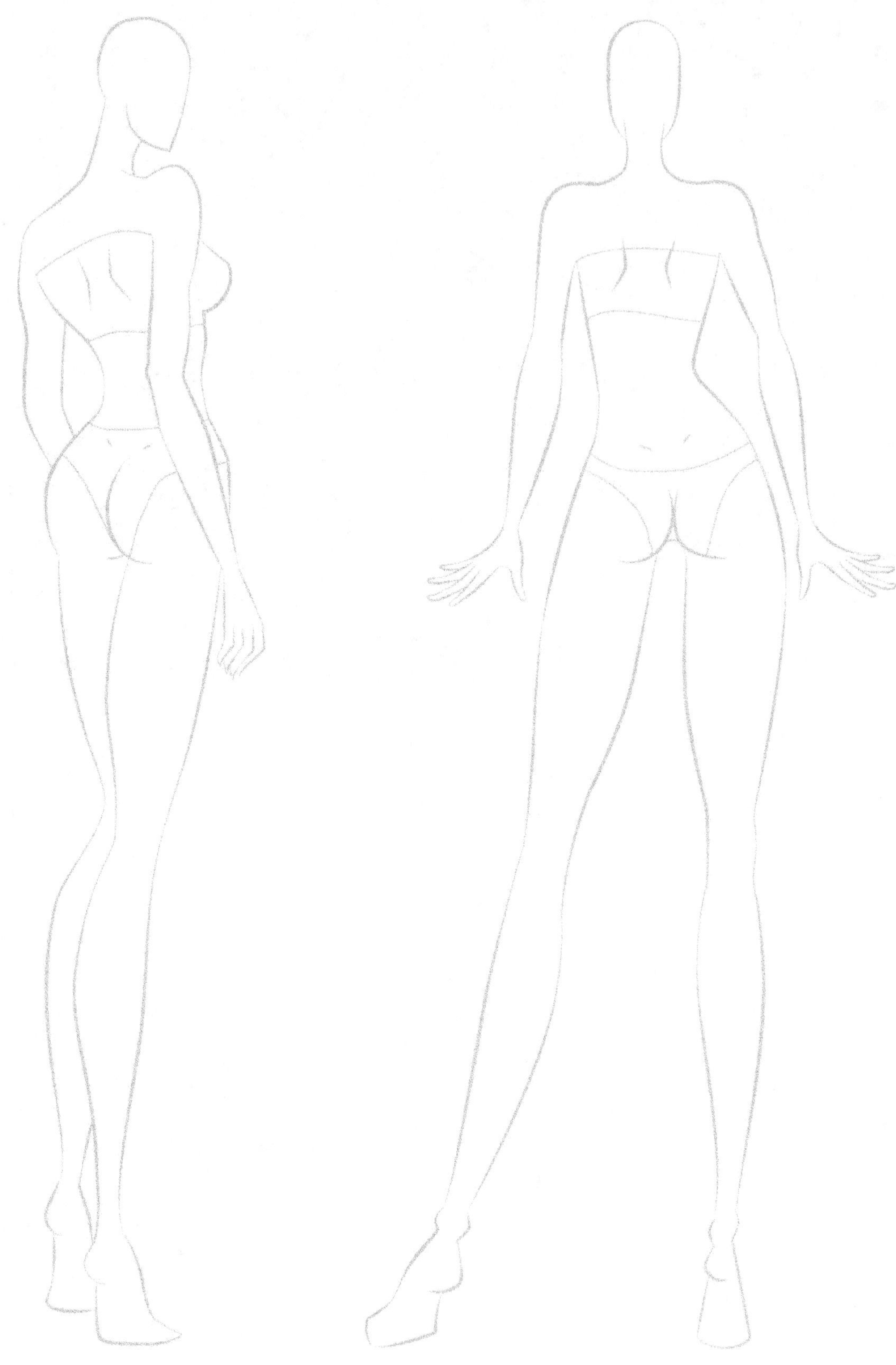

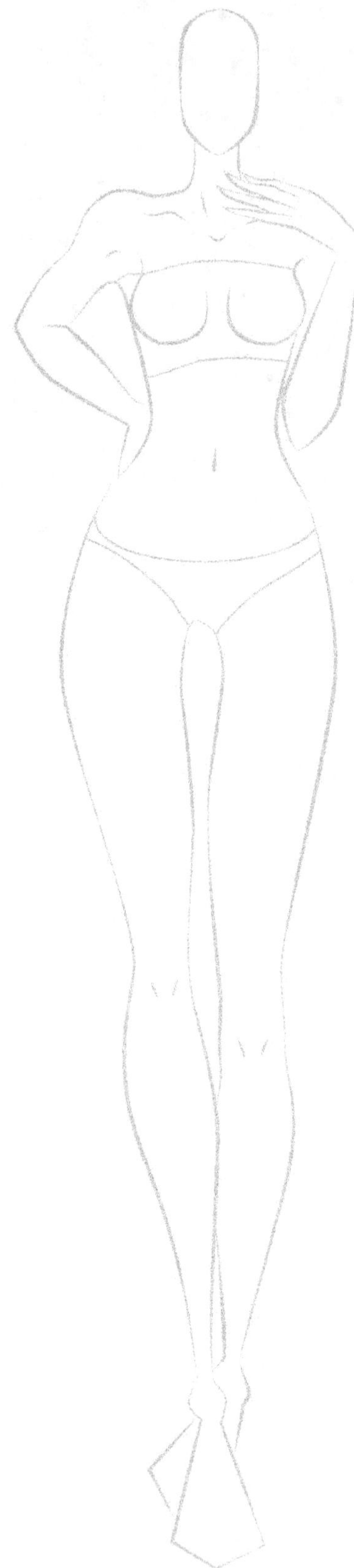

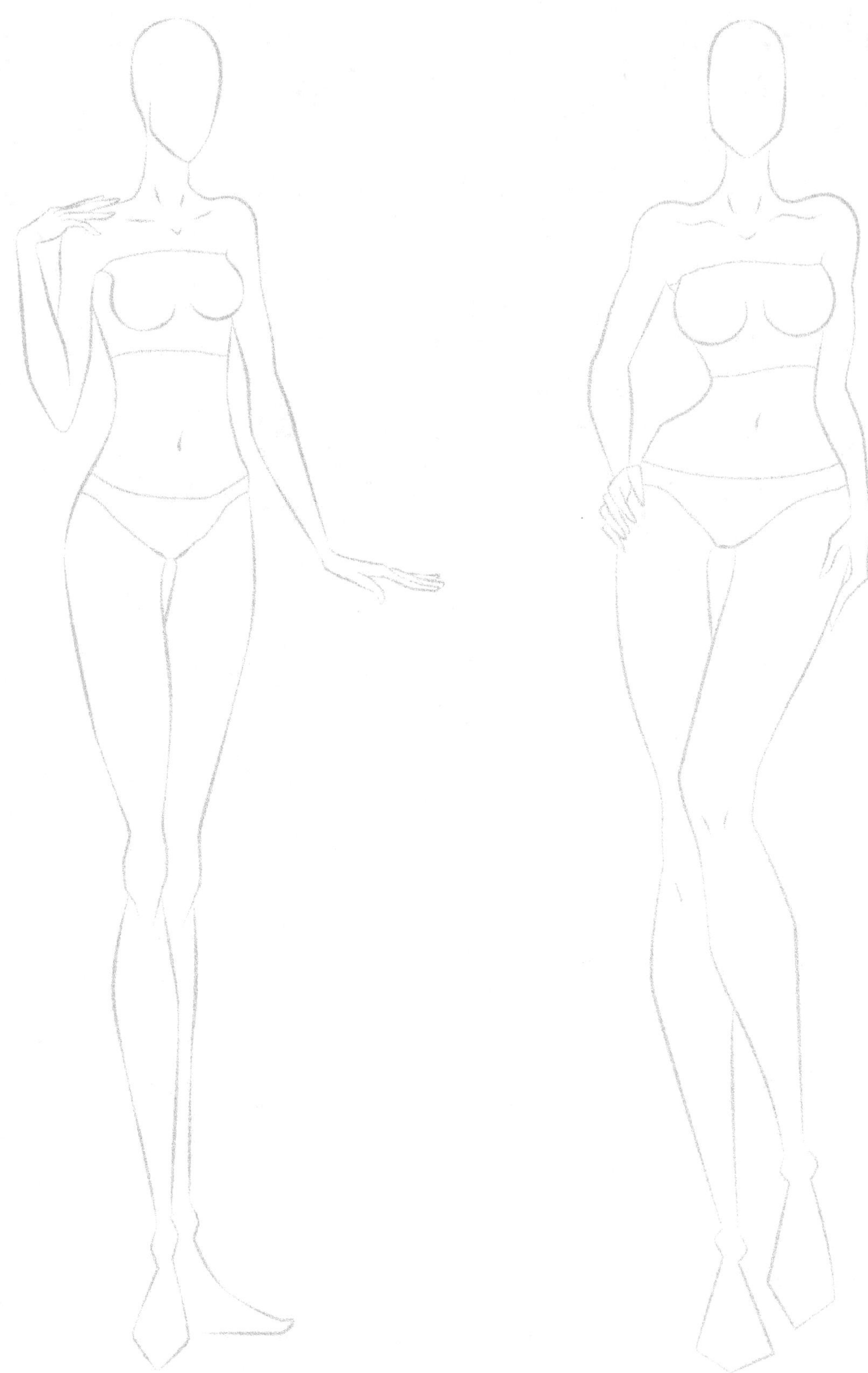

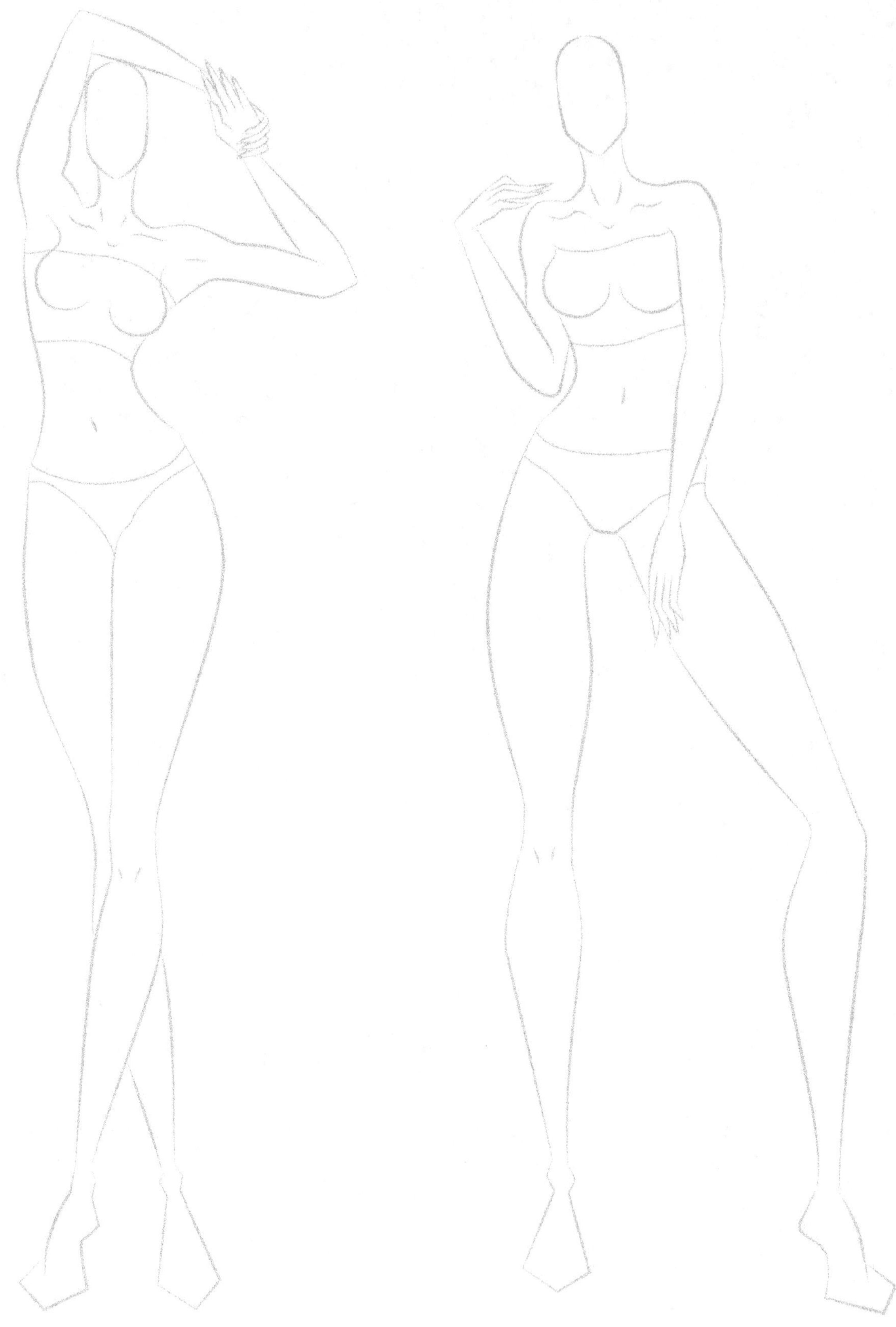

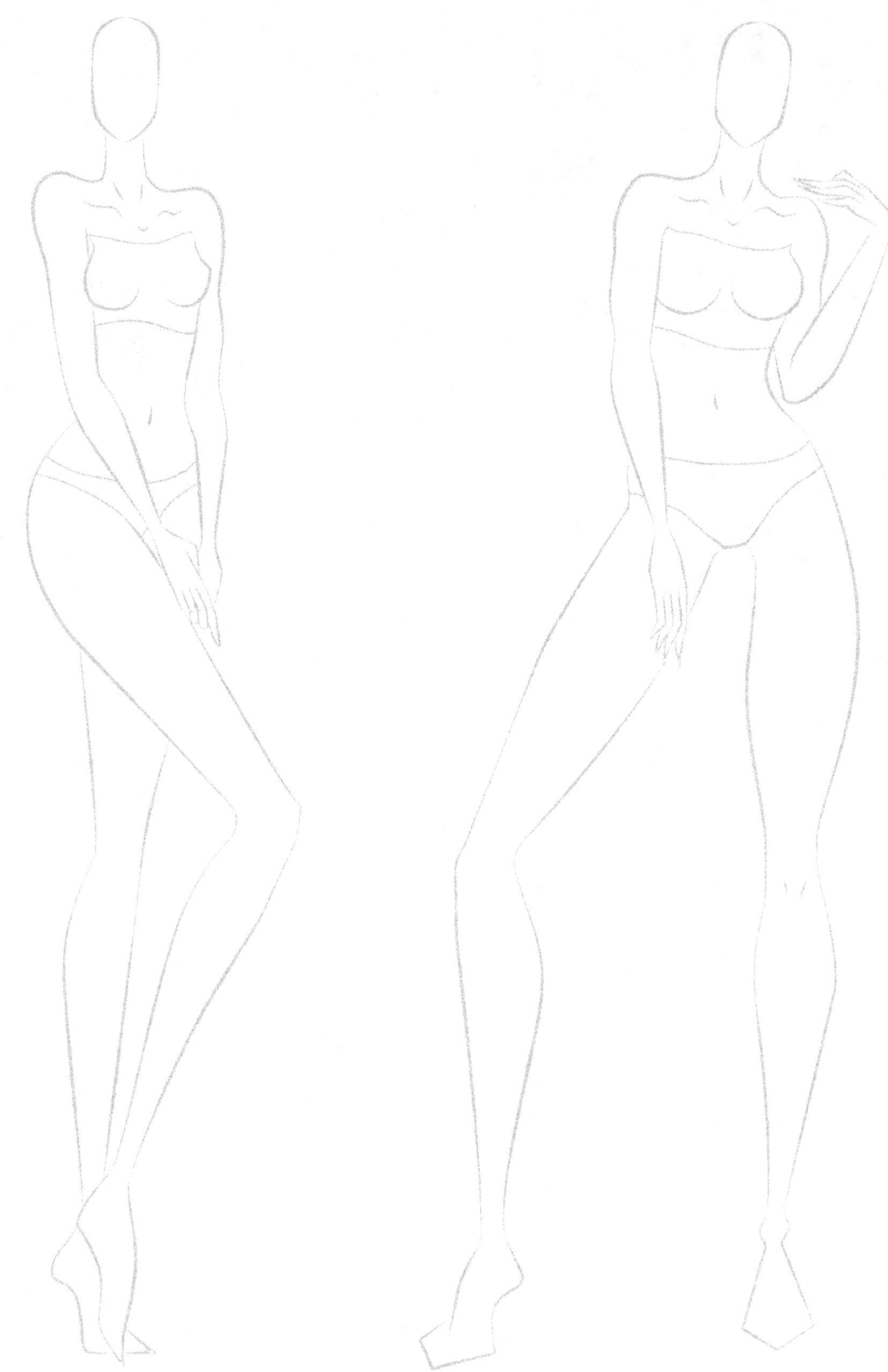

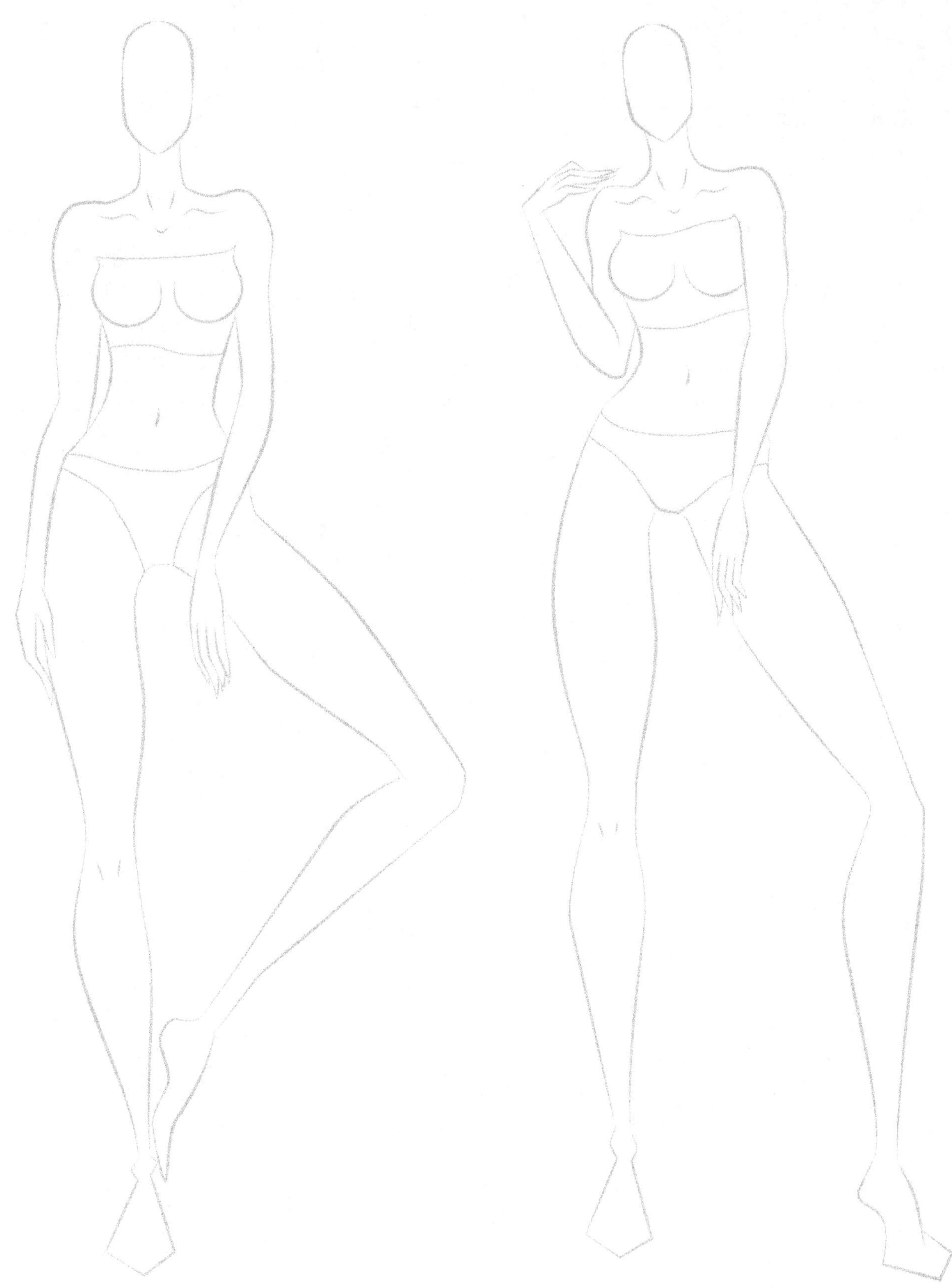

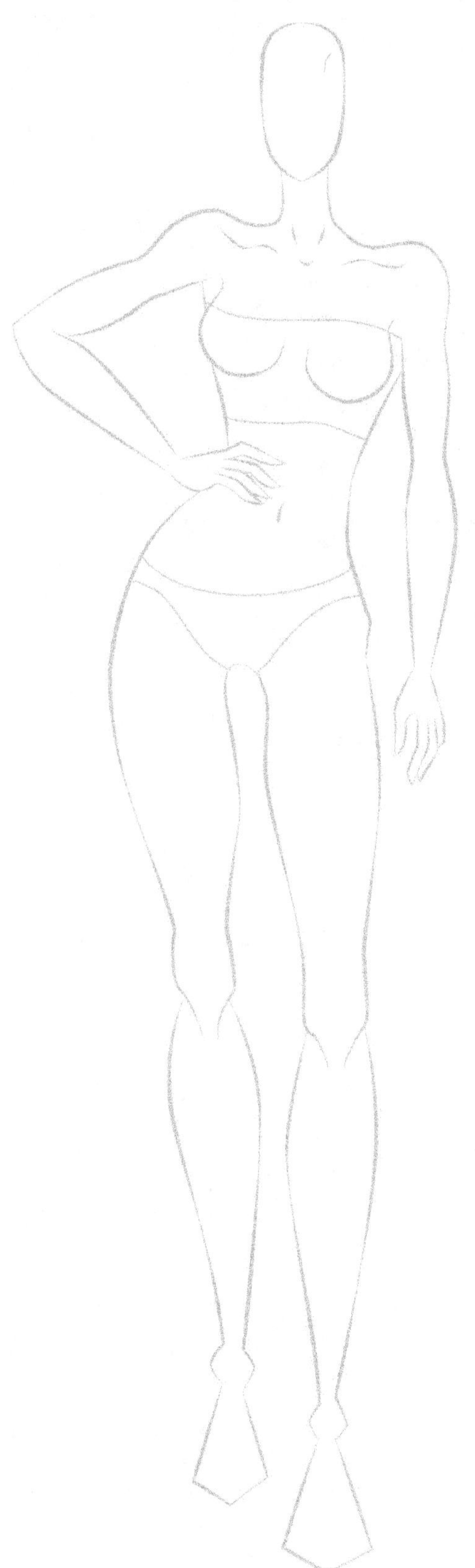

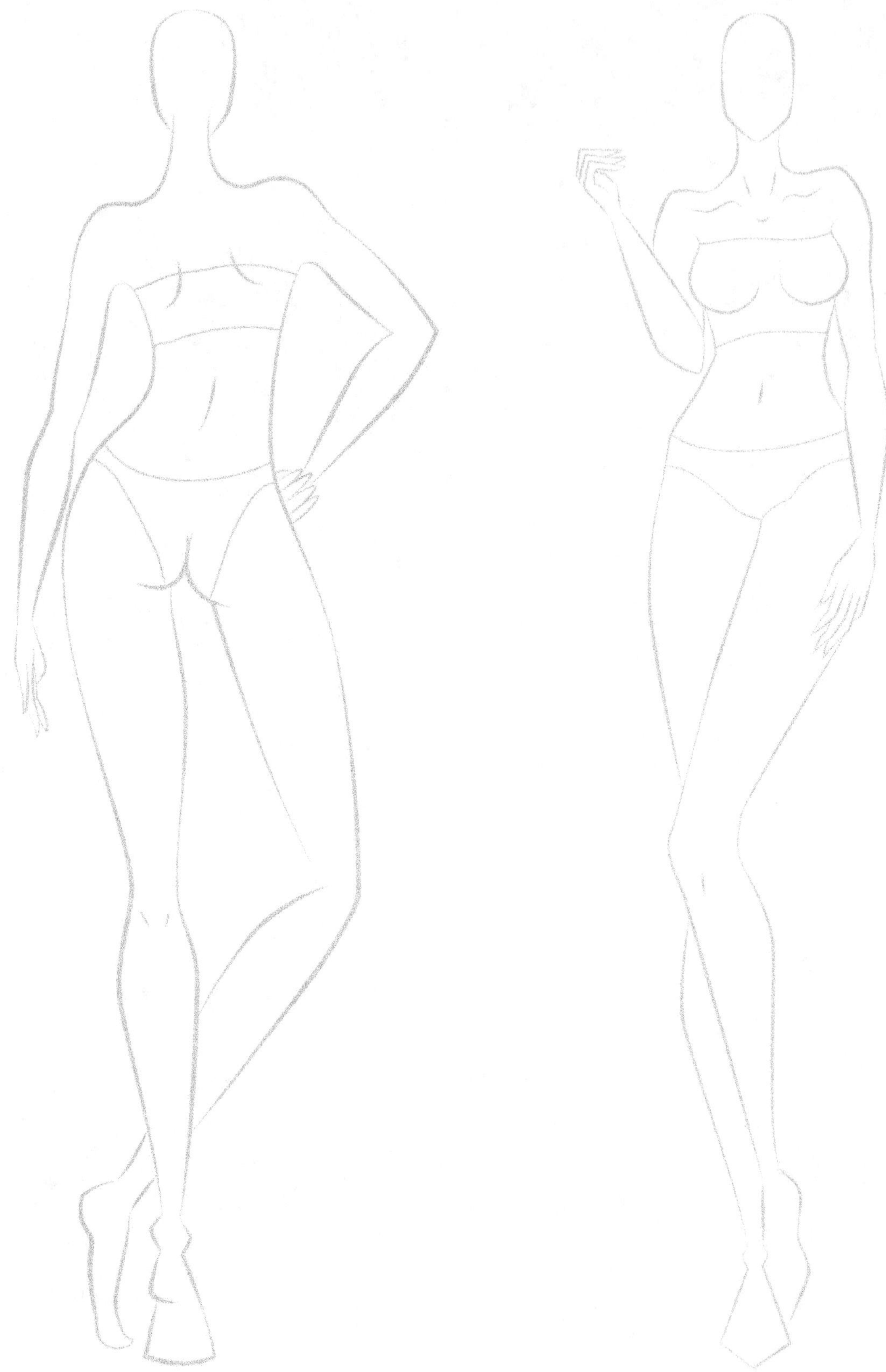

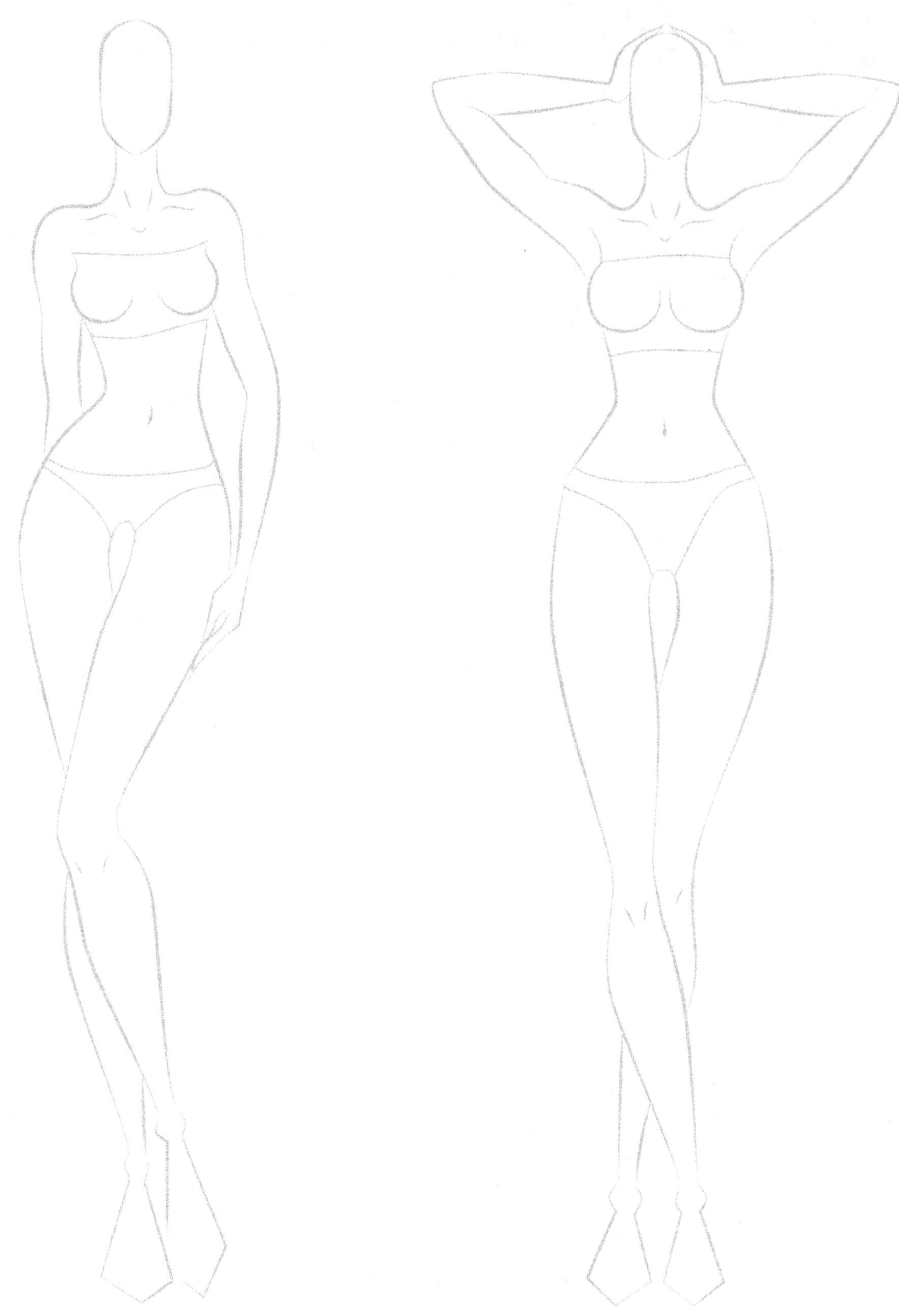

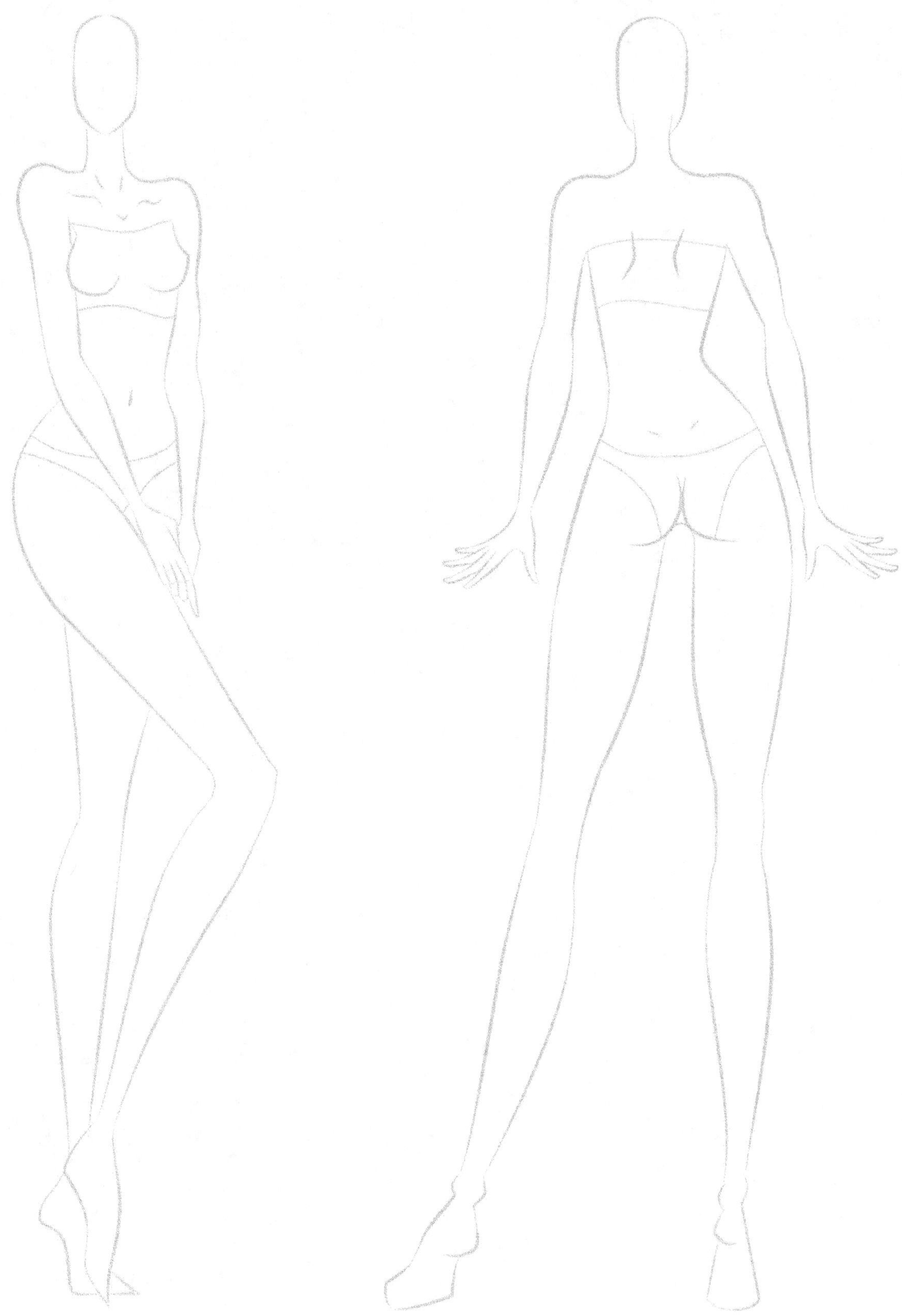

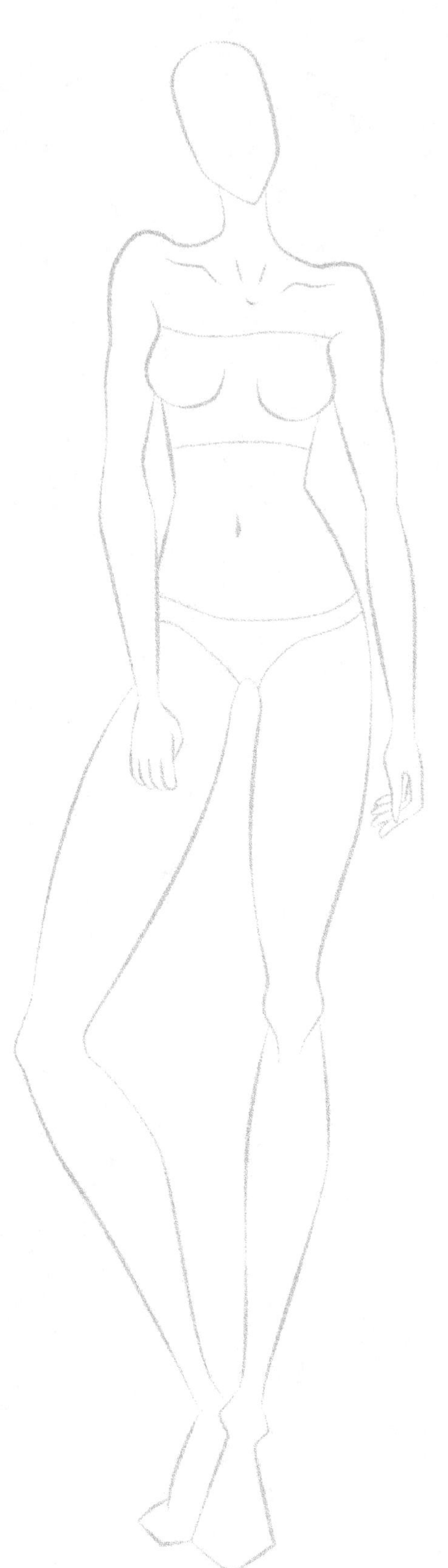

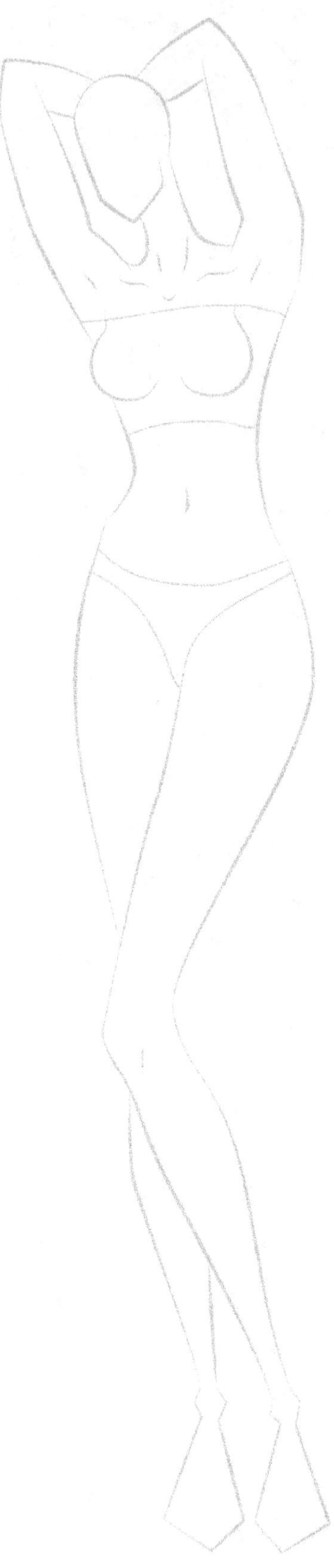

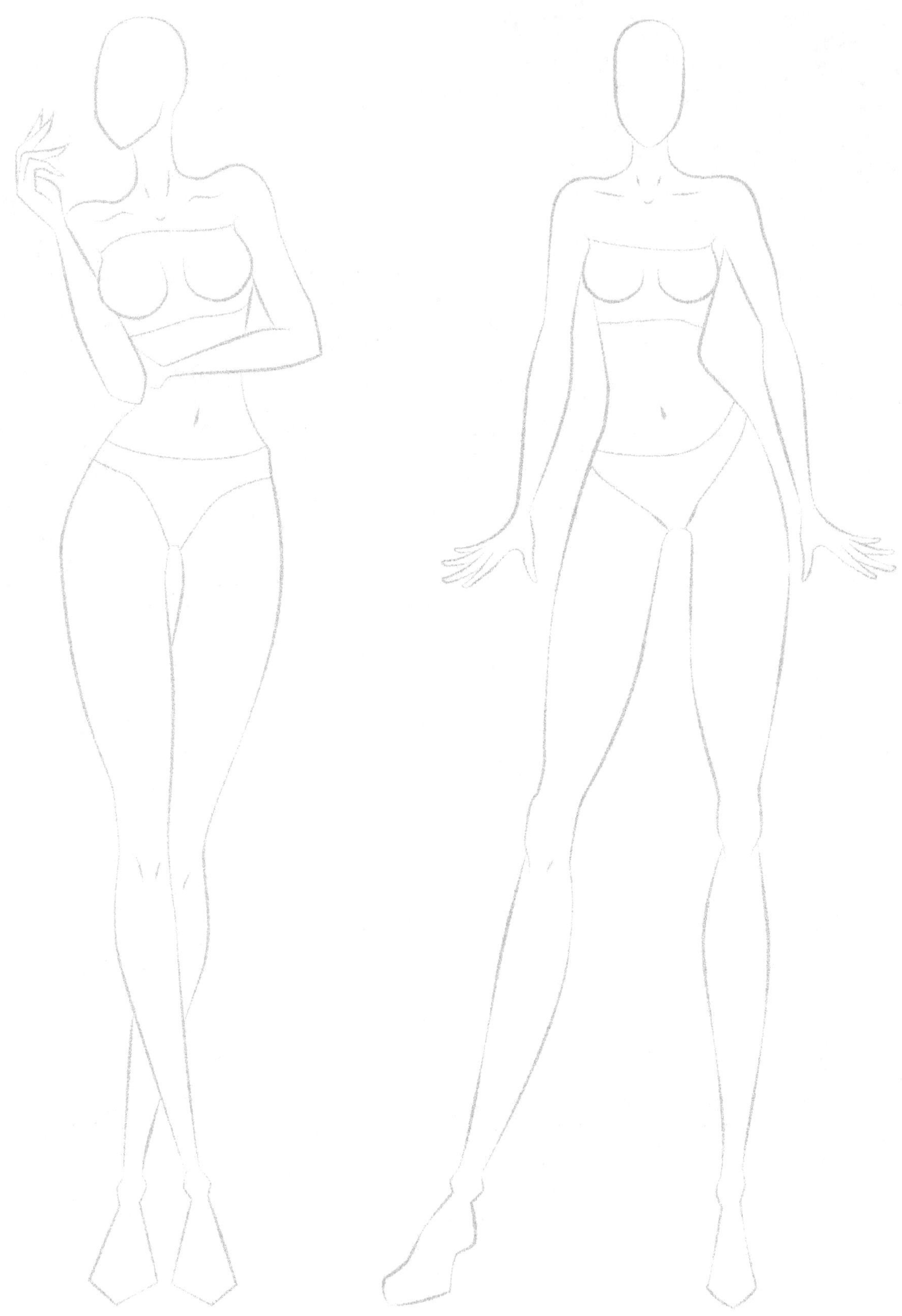

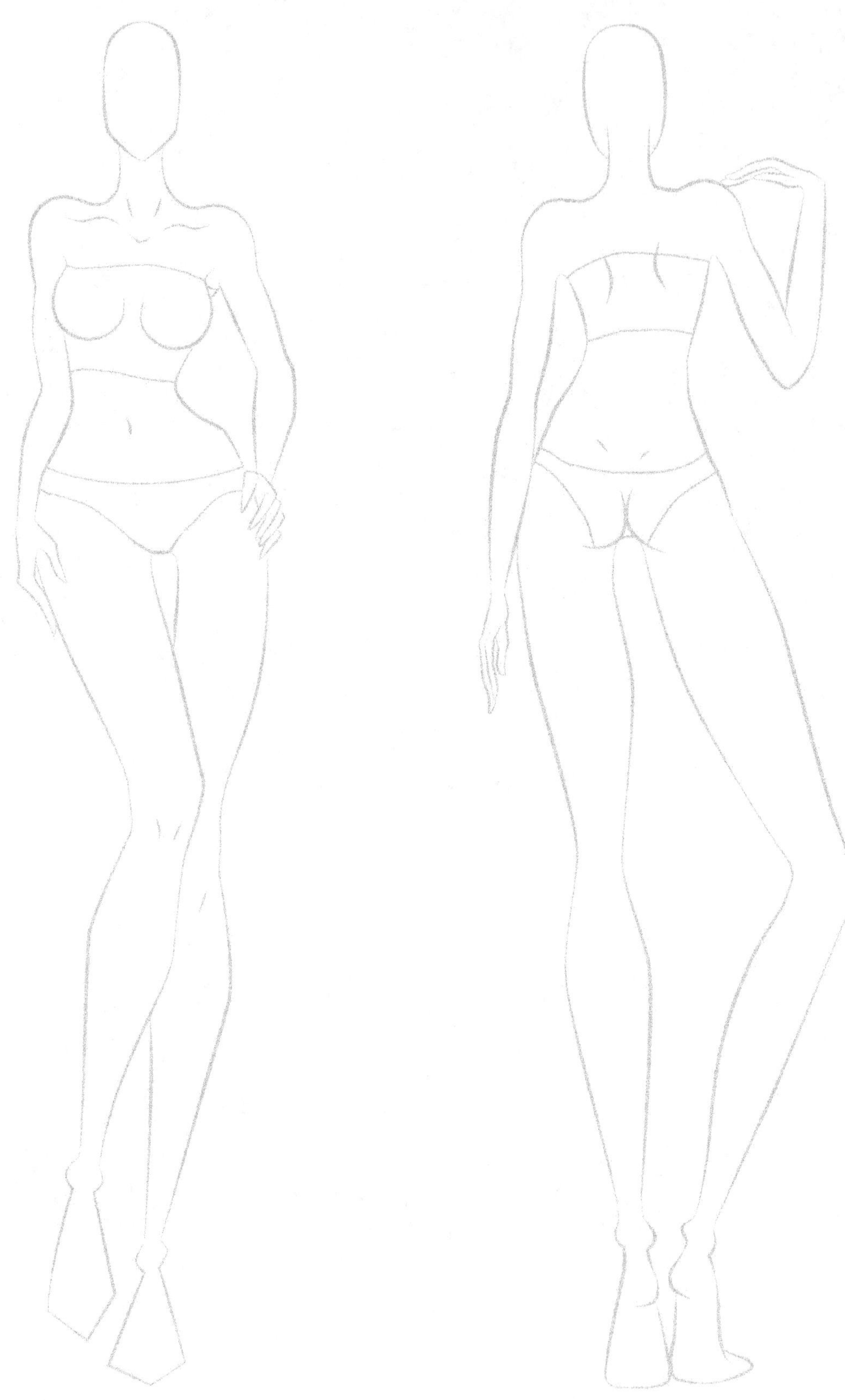

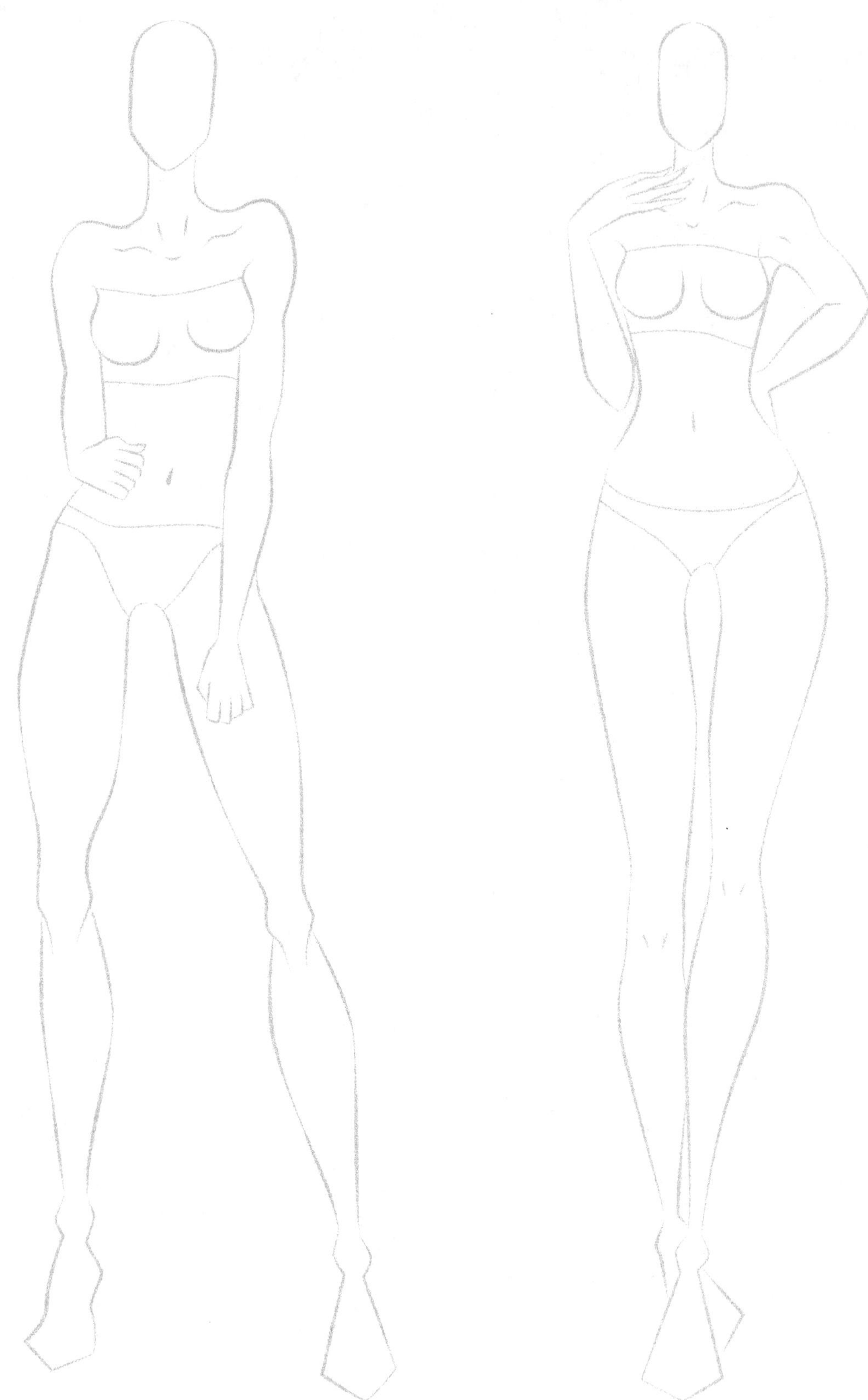

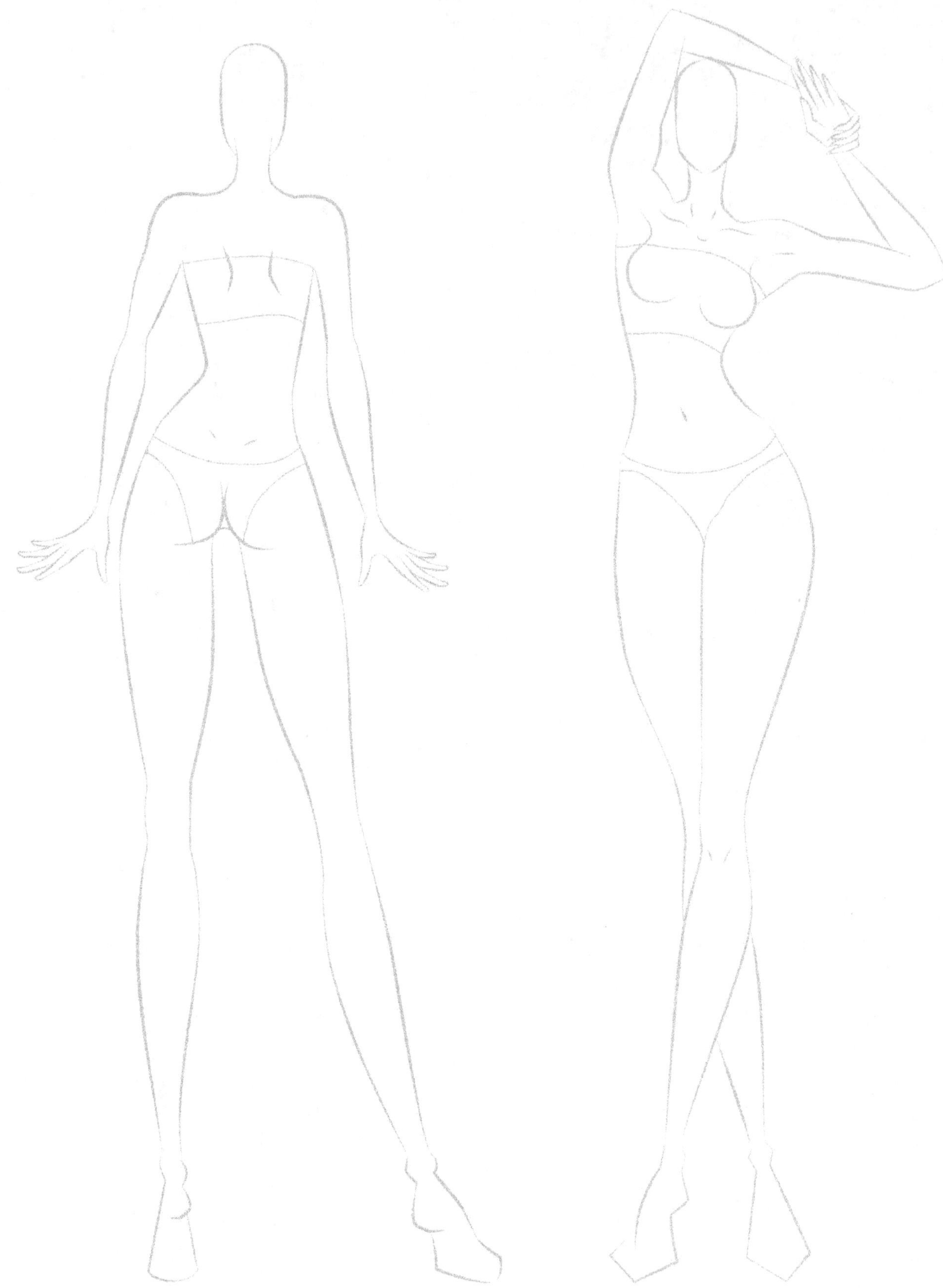

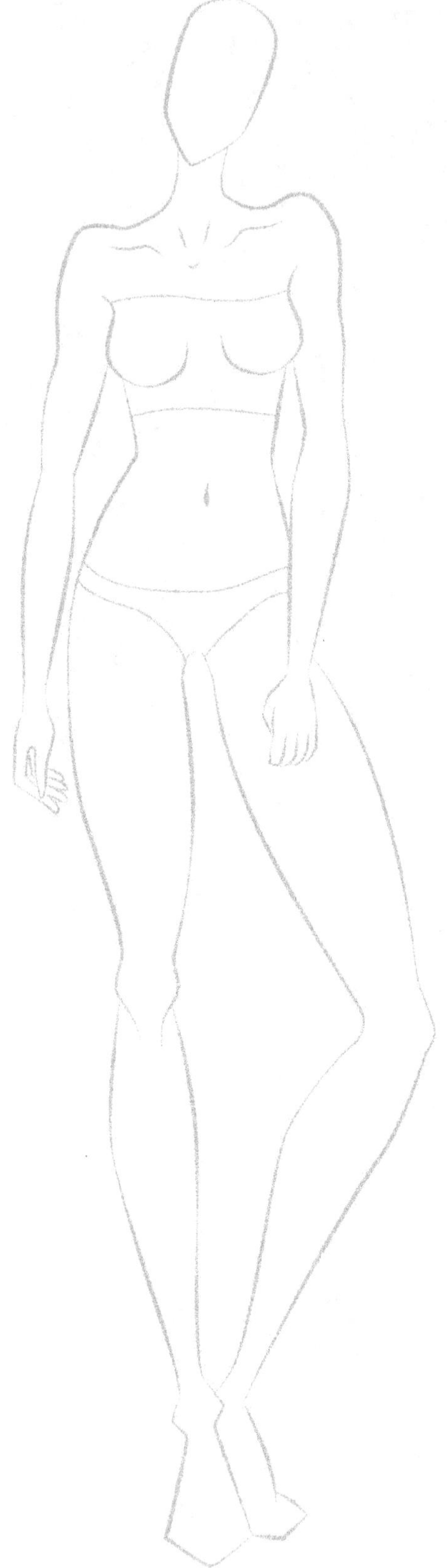

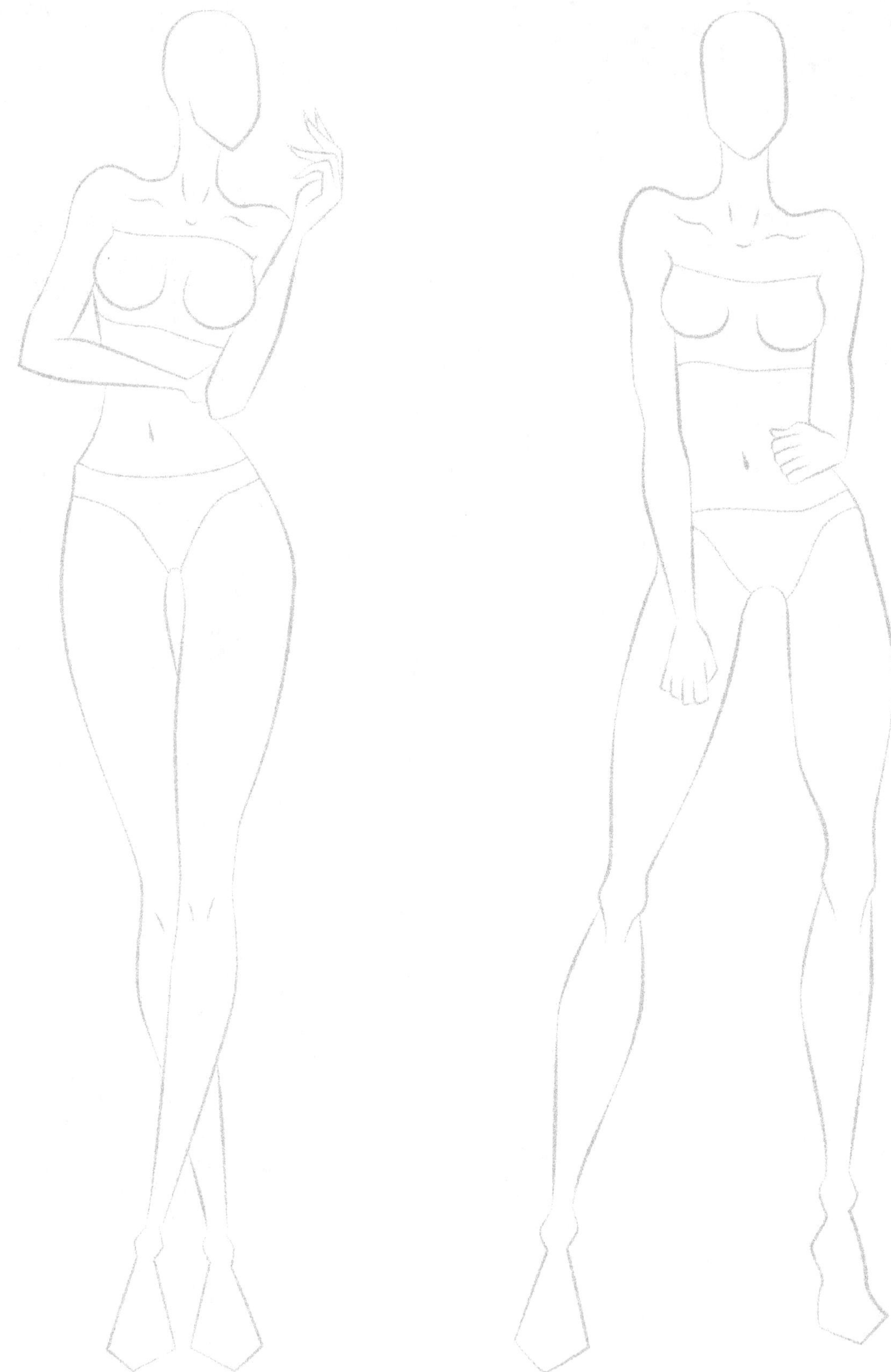